TABLE OF CONTENTS

i

ii

ISLAM: A VICTIM OF TERRORISM

Violence is one of the facts of modern international relations, mainly after the First World War and the devastating result of that war. The casualties and the destruction of that war had never been seen before. At the same time, violence is a corner stone of the element of terrorist crime, and a distinctive form of political crime, whether this terrorist crime is on the international or local level. Consequently, terrorism is the result of deviation of political, economical or ideological beliefs, or can be a combination of two or more of these beliefs.

Today, there are many religious groups accused of terrorist acts in the world. One of these religions is Islam. Islam is the last heavenly religion and one of the three major religions: Judaism, Christianity, and Islam, which will be examined in this paper. The western media for a long period of time has tried to mark the Islamic faith as a religion promoting hostility, violence, and terrorism, all carried out in the name of God. This got worse after the tragic attack on the United States that took place on September 11, 2001 by Islamic militants. A detailed examination of Islam, its history and tenets, will reveal that the religion is not the cause of terrorism, but a victim of terrorism.

WHAT IS ISLAM AND ITS ORIGINS?

In the Islamic faith, the prophet Abraham is the father of the three heavenly religions: Judaism, Christianity and Islam. Abraham had two sons, Ishmael and Isaac. Ishmael is the son of Abraham from his wife Hager, and Isaac is the son from his wife Sarah. Abraham received an order from God to take his wife Hager and their son Ishmael to Mecca on the Arabian Peninsula. After a time, Ishmael became the father of the Arabs, and Isaac who stayed in Palestine, became the father of the Hebrews. The Arabs and the Jews are both from the same Semitic stock.[1] The descendants of Isaac (Hebrews) were very stubborn and hard to keep faith, so God continually sent the prophets to them carrying the message of Abraham. Moses received the new message of Judaism. Judaism was the message of several prophets for the Hebrews who became Jews. But they continued to mistreat the prophets to the point of killing them. Not only were the Jews guilty of persecuting their prophets during their lifetime, but they also spared no effort to slander them after their deaths.[2]

God sent Jesus Christ with a new message. But the Jews did not accept the message of Jesus and Christianity. Even though they were Bani Israel (children of Israel) by birth, the Jews furiously disowned John and Jesus Christ as heretics because of the universal message they preached.[3] The Jews believed that the Messiah should be a "liberator" of the Jewish nation that was seeking to free itself from the yoke of the Roman Empire. Since Jesus message was offered to the Romans and other gentiles, he did not conform the Jewish Image of the messiah. Christianity was the last message to the Jews, and Jesus was the last messenger descending from Isaac.

The Arabs practiced the faith of Abraham and Ishmael for a long time. Idols were introduced to the Arabs by Amr Bin Luhai, a chief of Kuza'a tribe, one of the dominant tribes of Mecca. Amr Bin Luhai was renowned for his righteousness, charity, reverence, and care for the religion, and was granted unreserved love and obedience by his tribesmen. He came back from a trip to Syria where he had seen people worship idols. He approved of this phenomenon and believed it to be righteous since Syria was the locus of messengers and scriptures. He brought with him an idol (Hupal) which he placed in the middle of Al-Kabah, the sacred temple for the whole Arab nation which was built by the prophet Abraham and his son Ishmael, and summoned people to worship it.[4]Hupal, a material representation of God, was the first idol known to the Arabs

From the time of Abraham and Ishmael, an Arab performs the Hajj (Pilgrimage) to Mecca every year, to practice some of the rituals of Abraham's and Ishmael's religion. From that time, the Arabs started to add more idols, but it was not like Hupal which was in the shape of a man. The new idols were in different shapes, but never in the human or animal figures. The Arabs believe in God as the mighty lord and the creator of every physical thing. The Arabs believe that such idols or fraudulent gods, would bring them nearer to Allah, lead them to Him, and mediate with Him for their sake.[5]The Quran (Koran)states: "we worship them only that they may bring us near to Allah"[6]The majority of Arabs worship God through these idols. Some Arabs cling to Abraham's religion, and some convert to Christianity or Judaism.

The Quraysh tribe was the direct descendant of Ishmael and performed the duties of the custodians of the Al-Kabah temple. From Quraysh, a man named Mohammed received a message from God. That message was Islam. The word Islam in the Arabic language means peace. The literal meaning of Islam is submission to God. Islam literally means peace through submission to the will of God.[7]Islam simply requires people to worship one God and to abandon the worship of the idols. Islam calls for good manners and goodness between humans. It calls for goodness and kindness to animals and all creatures. It was the last heavenly religion that was revealed to humanity.

Islam is based on five pillars. The first is to acknowledge that there is no lord except God (Allah), and Mohammed is his prophet and messenger. The second is to perform prayers and piety to God. The third is fasting during the month of Ramadan. The fourth is the paying alms

(Zkaht). The fifth is performing the Hajj (Pilgrimage) to Mecca for those who are physically capable.

Even though these pillars are the foundation of the Islamic faith, Islam is a sequel of the previous religions (Christianity and Judaism) and also calls for the rightfulness of humans and kindness to each other. As in all religions, the three Abrahamec religions--Islam, Judaism, and Christianity--promote peace, love and harmony among mankind. The theme of these religions is peace as long as there is no oppression or injustice. The Quran states,

> "...fight in the way of Allah with those who fight with you, and do not exceed the limits, surely Allah does not love those who exceed the limits."[8]

In a closer look into the three religions, similarity appears in the reason for the message which calls for worshipping one mighty God and abandoning any other God. Indeed, both the Islamic and Judeo-Christian faiths contain common religious and historical parameters. For example both faiths contemplate the "second coming" of the Messiah and his defeat of the false Messiah, they contain common prophecies, and their history rests in the region of the Middle East.

In the Islamic faith, followers believe in God, his Angels, his holy books, his messengers, fate, and in the judgment day. If a person does not believe in any one of these tenets, he could not be a Muslim. This belief is expressed in books. Those are the Torah, the book of Moses; the bible, the book of Jesus; and the Quran, the book of Mohamed. They are all from God and they are holy books. The belief in messengers is believing that God sent messengers to humanity from Adam, father of mankind, through Noah, Abraham, Moses, Jesus, and Mohamed, and other prophets that God talked about in the holy books.

Islam is a religion of laws that involve every aspect of human life from personal hygiene to personal relations. These laws address family and individual duties, functioning of societies, civil laws and relations between nation-states. One can say that Islam is not just a religion, it is a way of life. Islam is not merely a system of belief and worship, or just a compartment of life, so to speak, distinct from other compartments that are the concern of nonreligious authorities administering nonreligious laws. Rather, it is the whole of life and its rules, including civil, criminal, and even what we would call constitutional law.[9]

In the Quran, Islam calls upon its followers to respect other religions and their followers by offering protection for their lives, their properties, and their worshiping temples. Also they call people to Islam by means of persuasion, and not to force Islam upon them. The Quran states:

3

"There is no compulsion in religion; truly the right way has become clearly distinct from error; therefore, whoever disbelieves in the evil and believes in Allah he indeed has laid hold on the firmest handle, which shall not break off, and Allah is Hearing, Knowing."[10]

The prophet gives an example of this by living next to a Jewish neighbor. He conducted business relations with his Jewish neighbors of Medina, declaring that the Jews of Medina are part of the nation (Umma). After receiving a commitment from the Medina Jews that they will not fight him or support others against the Muslim community in Medina, the prophet issued a constitution declaring that the three groups: Muhajirin (Muslims migrating from Mecca), Ansar (Muslims from Medina), and Jews, constituted a single (Umma) nation distinct from other peoples, and bound by a common defense pact against external aggression.[11] The prophet went further by marrying a Muslim woman of Christian origin. His wife Maria was a Coptic Christian slave from Egypt when she converted to Islam. He also took as a wife, Saphiah, who was a Muslim woman of Jewish origin. The Quran calls the followers of Christianity and Judaism the people of the book, even complimenting the faithful ones in several verses, indicating that Islam accepts other religions. For example, the Quran states:

"They are not all alike; of the followers of the Book there is an upright party; they recite Allah's communications in the nighttime and they adore (Him). They believe in Allah and the last day, and they enjoin what is right and forbid the wrong and they strive with one another in hastening to good deeds, and those are among the good. And whatever good they do, they shall not be denied it, and Allah knows those who guard (against evil)."[12]

The diplomacy of the prophet in itself was a lesson in international relations. The prophet kept the political and human relations out of the religious constraints as long as they did not conflict with the principles of the Islamic faith. The prophet asked his companions (sahaba) not to assume any religious authority when concluding treaties with other parties, but rather to let such agreements be governed by political and human consideration.[13]

Upon the death of the prophet Mohamed in 632AD, the first caliph Abu Bakr (632-634AD) succeeded him, and was then followed by caliph Omar Bin Al-Kataab (634-644AD). A non-Muslim Persian killer assassinated Caliph Omar. Caliph Othman Bin Afan (644-656AD) succeeded Omar, but the hands of Muslim rebels killed him. Othman's death marked the beginning of internal violence in Islamic history. The fourth caliph Ali Bin Abetaleb (656-616AD) succeeded Othman. The first five years of Caliph Ali's reign was an era of unrest and wars between Muslims themselves. It also marked the creation of Islamic sects where the followers of Ali were called the Shiite and the followers of Maawiah Bin Abu Sufian were called Sunni. Also during his era, the Arab Islamic Empire started to expand outside the Arabian Peninsula.

Prior to the Islamic Era, the Eastern Roman Byzantine and Persian Empires were the dominant hegemonies in the world, and had a strong influence on the Arabic kingdom in the north. The Gasasenah Kingdom was under the protection of the Eastern Roman Byzantine, and the Manatherah Kingdom was under the protection of the Persian Empire. When most of the Arabic tribes in the Arabian Peninsula converted to Islam, they united for the first time in Arab history. With the Arabs united, the Islamic state became strong. The neighboring Arabic kingdoms in the north (what is known today as Syria and Iraq), and the Eastern Roman Byzantine and Persian empires, feared the rising power of the Islamic state. Clash was inevitable between the Eastern Roman Byzantine and Persian Empires and the Arab Islamic state.

In the last days of the prophet Mohamed, he sent messages to the leader of the Persian Empire and to the leaders of the Christian Eastern Roman Byzantine Empire, and the Copts in Egypt and Ethiopia, calling them to Islam. The Christan leaders treated and returned the messengers with respect, declining to accept the call. The prophet sent an army of three thousand to fight the Gassany kingdom, but that campaign did not achieve its goal. The death of Mohamed delayed the second campaign, but the first caliph Abu Bakr went ahead and sent an army of forty thousand men to fight the Gassany kingdom. Byzantine supported their Gassany allies in the war against the Islamic state. That war continued during the era of the four caliphs. Thus the Islamic state took the call for Islam as the main reason for the fight with the neighboring Persian and Eastern Roman Byzantine.

The Ummayad Dynasty started the first monarchy in the Islamic Arab political system. Maawiah Bin Abu Sufian was appointed as the first governor of Syria by his cousin Caliph Othman Bin Afan. Following Othman's death, Maawiah asked Caliph Ali to bring Othman's killers to justice. Ali's failure to arrest and try Othman's killers became a cause of war between Ali and Maawiah. Ali, in an effort to stop the hostilities and end the resulting bloodbath, agreed to negotiate with Maawiah an end to the war. Both Ali and Maawiah appointed their respective representatives for the negotiations to end the war. The two representatives met and they agreed that in order to end the war the two leaders should be removed and that the Umma (a popular assembly) should hold an election for a new Caliph. However, Maawiah's representative tricked Ali's representative to speak first and declare Ali's "removal" from his position of power at the Caliphate (essentially this trick prompted Ali's "involuntary retirement" by his own representative). Maawiah's representative then declared Maawiah as the new Caliph.

Caliph Ali accepted the decision and stepped-down from the Caliphate and went back to Medina. But his followers did not accept that decision and war started again. After the murder of Caliph Ali, the followers wanted his sons to continue the Caliphate. The war ended with the massacre of the sons of the Caliph Ali, and the grandchildren of the prophet Mohamed. That war was in Karbala, in south Iraq.

After the defeat of Ali's sons in Karbala, the opposition movement turned into an underground movement working against the Ummaih dynasty. The Ummaih dynasty countered that movement by persecuting the members and followers of the Shiite movement. As described in the earliest Arabic historical narratives, they formed a group with a political and, in the initial stage, largely a personal choice, as the basis for their group action. In time, the word (Shiite) came to denote one of the major divisions of the Islamic religion community. [14] The political opposition was so deep that the leaders of that movement started their own religious sect to distinguish themselves from the rest of the Ummaih followers. What started as political opposition turned in time to a division into religious sects of the same faith.

For the strategic protection of the Islamic state, the Muslim leaders saw the Mediterranean Sea as a buffer zone between the Islamic world and the Christian world (Europe). But the self-interest and the love of power by the caliphs of the Ummaih and Abassy dynasties drove the Islamic conquering armies to Europe and Asia in an attempt to expand the Islamic state. It was not until the caliph Omar Bin Abdualaziz put an end to the Islamic expansion, reverting to defending its existing territories from that time on.

A look at the history of Islam shows that it is a religion from God based on peace through submission to the to the will of God, where all living creatures are treated with kindness. When violence has appeared in its history, it was based not on the tenets of Islam, but on the greed and lust for power by those who did not truly accept its teachings.

THE DEFINITION OF TERRORISM

According to the Geneva treaty signed in 1937, acts of terrorism are "criminal acts directed against a state and intended or calculated to create a state of terror in the minds of particular persons or groups of persons or the general public"[15]

The definition of terrorism according to the Islamic Fiqh (Islamic knowledge) Academy (IFA) (a subsidiary organ of the Organization of the Islamic Conference (OIC)), at the Islamic Summit Conference held in Mecca (Saudi Arabia), terrorism is defined as the acts of aggression committed by individuals, groups or states directed against persons or the general public (their faith, body, mind, property and dignity). It includes terror, threats, killing without just cause, and hijacking, intended to terrorize the public, or threaten them, their freedom and their safety. It includes threats against the environment, public or private property, and natural resources. The Quran states:

> "When he turns his back, his aim everywhere is to spread mischief through the earth and destroy crops and cattle. But Allah loveth not mischief."[16]

The punishment of such acts in the Islamic law is also severe. Again, The Quran states:

> "The punishment of those who wage war against Allah and His apostle and strive to make mischief in the land is only this, that they should be murdered or crucified or their hands and their feet should be cut off on opposite sides or they should be imprisoned; this shall be as a disgrace for them in this world, and in the hereafter they shall have a grievous chastisement."[17]

IS THERE SUCH PHENOMENA AS RELIGIOUS TERRORISM?

A reward is what every one is looking for in return for doing something, it is human nature. This reward is either materialist in nature or moralist. It drives people to do whatever has been asked of them to do. The materialists (mercenary soldiers, employees, businessmen, and other occupations), get their reward from money, wealth and power. The moralist (priests, some soldiers, freedom fighters, and charity workers) gets their reward from more noble causes. One can apply these two classifications to criminal activities, where thieves or organized crime look for money and power as their reward. The terrorist performs his criminal acts in the name of religion, driven by his or her faith, which becomes the "noble cause" reward. This is a very important point. The leaders of any terrorist organization realize this point and enforce it in the minds of their followers. The only capital investment on the leaders part is some promises that the follower will get to heaven after his or her death. For any analyst studying terrorism, he must keep in mind that a terrorist believes that if he succeeds in his mission, he will be rewarded. If the follower fails, he will still be rewarded because even though he failed, he was still acting in the name of God. Ironically, if one kills a terrorist, one is actually doing him a favor by letting him get his reward sooner. This idea is not exclusive to a particular religion or faith. It is a wide spread practice in almost every religion or faith, including: Judaism, Podasime, Hinduism, Sikhism, Christianity, and Islam. The scholars of the fundamental organizations use some verses of the holy books to justify their actions and aggression against societies or against noncombatant nations or people. It's the not the religions that change, it's the people who interpret the religions. The practice of religion changes because men change it.[18]

THE EMERGENCE OF ISLAMIC EXTREMISM AND RESULTING EFFECTS

As a result of European occupation of the Middle East and the Islamic world, the British and French instituted misguided policies (Sykes-Picot Accord of 1916) which divided the Arab world into petty states. The resulting boundaries would work to ensure conflict within the region for a long time to come. Further complications developed with the inauspicious promise of the Foreign Minster of Great Britain, Sir Arthur Balfour, in 1917. He promised to establish a homeland for the Jews in Palestine. In 1948, a United Nations resolution lead by the United States and Great Britain, created the state of Israel in Palestine, implanting Israel in the heart of the Arab world. This in turn created a problem and resulting tragedy: Palestinian refugees. The British Prime Minster, Winston Churchill said, "the creation of a state of a European style in Palestine will act as a buffer zone to protect the British interests in the Middle East and the Suez Canal"[19]

The conflicts between India and the Islamic nation of Pakistan, and Iraq and Iran on border issues, are all a result of British policies, policies which made wars inevitable in those regions. The impact of British imperialism was acknowledged by the Foreign Minster of Great Britain, Mr. Jack Strow when he said, "The colonialism past of Great Britain is responsible for most of the current conflicts in the Middle East, and between India and Pakistan"[20]

The result of these situations was the birth of several freedom fighter organizations. They started as armed struggles to gain independence. One of the first organizations was Al-Ikhwan Al-Muslimun (Muslim brothers) in Egypt. A religion teacher named Hasan Al-Banna founded this organization in Egypt in 1928.[21] Al-Ikhwan Al-Muslimun was established in response to a number of events which took place simultaneously: the fall of the Islamic khilafa (Caliphat) in 1924, the colonization of the Muslim world by western powers, and the spread of westernization in Muslim countries.[22] These organizations were marked by western government and media as terrorist organizations, and their struggle, or acts, were called terrorism. This attitude created the anti-Islamic movement in the West, and the term "Islamic terror" came into existence.

In the 1920's, the political goals and objectives of most Islamic movements or militant groups were clear and agreed upon by most Muslims; it was the liberation of the Arab and Islamic world from the foreign occupation. After the independence from colonizing powers, most Arab and Islamic governments or organizations or people joined these movements in the effort to regain the Islamic state, and to free the Islamic World from western occupation. After

8

independence, a lot of the Islamic movement lost the support of the public due to the lack of an Islamic political agenda or program to govern an Islamic state. The result was that most Islamic movements did not move in the political arena to fill the gap in the leadership that was created after the departure of the occupying colonial power. Unfortunately that gap was filled with corrupt leadership which was working for the occupation powers.

The Islamic movements started all over, but this time the struggle was against local Muslim governments. This situation forced local military leadership to step in on the political side and take over the government. Examples of such military coups include: Egypt in 1952; Sudan in 1958, 1969, and 1989; Syria in 1949 and 1961; Libya in 1969; and Iraq in 1936, 1963; the Baath party in 1968; and ending with Saddam Hussein's takeover in 1979. The military governments started to suppress the Islamic movements in the name of anti-terrorism. They imposed martial law in a violent way and without any consideration of human rights.

Violence leads to more violence. The Islamic movements turned to the Quran to find answers to what went wrong and why they failed in what was supposed to be a success. They followed the path of Islam, but they did not succeed in restoring the Islamic state. The scholars of the Islamic fundamental organizations did not acknowledge the problem. The problem was what they were preaching was not relevant to the nineteenth century. They did not comprehend that the world had changed since the time of the prophet. They did not recognize that the geopolitical landscape of the Arab and Islamic worlds had changed. To overcome the doubts of whether their religious-based ideological beliefs were a valid basis for their struggle, the Islamist movements started criticizing the way of life in the Muslim societies where these movements were active. They also started arguing that the life of Muslims must return to the ways of their ancestors. This approach unfortunately failed to recognize that although ways of life may change, they still need to be reconciled with the unchanging underlying beliefs of the Islamic faith. This requires a continuous in-depth and scholarly examination of the faith, and its application to the spiritual and materialist challenges of modern life. In other words, the Islamic faith and its relationship and application to modern life are a dynamic and not a static process. Islam certainly is not hateful in its essence but a disproportionate number of its current adherents thrive on controversy and need a heated argument to avoid the agony of self-knowledge.[23]

The point worth noticing in these organizations is when they are suppressed by government, the organization's reaction is to form into smaller fragments or subdivisions. In these smaller structures some of the survival elements establish new clusters. One of the main characteristics of every new subdivision is that it becomes more extreme and more violent. After president Abdelnaser of Egypt prosecuted the Al-Ikhwan Al-Muslimun by killing its leader and throwing its members in jail, new organizations came to the surface. A good example of these extreme groups is the Al Takfeer wa Al Hejrah. It was a part of Al-Ikhwan Al-Muslimun and believed that anyone who did not believe in their groups ideologies was not Muslim, but an Infidel. To this particular group, the entire Egyptian, as well as other Muslim nations, were infidels. Another example is the Jamat almuslimin (Muslims Group) who consider all the Arab state rulers as non-Muslims. It even went further when a member of Jamat almuslimin refused to pray to the Kaabah in Mecca because they considered that the Kaabah was under non-Islamic rule.[24] This ideology has spread to other countries, when a group of Saudi Islamic militants, lead by Juhiman Al-Otaibi, captured the holy mosque in Mecca in 1979 in an attempt to free the mosque from the Saudi Arabian government believing it was a non-Islamic government. Usama Bin laden has the same ideology regarding the Saudi government. Bin laden preaches replacing what he sees as non-Islamic regimes, such as Saudi Arabia, with ones which are more transparently founded on Islamic religious principles. He advocates regimes which act at all levels in accordance with Islamic principles, and which do not rely on political support from Western countries, particularly America.[25]

Some analysts also believe that some of these organizations have been created and/or used by foreign governments to influence Islamic and Arab governments, or to apply pressure to particular states or other organizations. An example of this is the Hamas organization, which was sponsored by the Israeli government from the 1970s until well into the 1980s. The Israeli government fostered the Muslim Brotherhood (and its offshoot, Hamas) in the occupied territories -- the same group that was later considered to be especially dangerous.[26] It was a part of the pressure applied on the Palestinian Liberation Organization (PLO) and its leader by drawing some of the support of the Palestinian people and dividing the unity of that nation into several organizations. It is also argued that the Israeli occupation itself helped to expand the influence of the Islamic movement. The Israeli reasoning was "to grant permission" for religious and Islamic movements to expand the areas of their activities and their support within the ranks of the Arab citizens. They hoped to undermine the influence of, and support for the Palestinian nationalist forces, especially those loyal to the PLO.[27] Other examples are the use of the Islamic movement to attack targets of the tourism industries in Egypt to destroy the Egyptian economy, and the attack against the Christian minority in an attempt to start a religious conflict between Muslims and Christians.

The United States used the Mujahedeen in Afghanistan after the Russians invaded that country. The United States and its allies in the Arabs world supported the Afghan Jihad against the communist Russian invasion. Members of a guerilla army "Mujahedeen" were also encouraged and armed by the United States. They were quickly forgotten when that war was over.[28] Upon the defeat of the Russian army and the end of the Russian occupation of Afghanistan, the Afghan civil war started. The Mujahedeen were frustrated from that war and had a dream of creating an Islamic state. But they saw that the Arab and Muslim states were working to escalate the civil war between two Islamic sects: the Taliban Sunni group, supported by Saudi Arabia, the United Arab Emirates and Pakistan; and the Northern alliance Shiite group, supported by Iran, and other western and eastern nations, trying to gain a political influence in Afghanistan. So the Mujahedeen retuned to their country and started to fight their government in what was known as the "Afghan Arab". It involved an estimated 5,000 trained Saudis, 3,000 Yemenis, 2,800 Algerians, 2,000 Egyptians and perhaps 2,000 Palestinians, Jordanians, Lebanese, Iranians and others.[29] Among them was Usama Bin laden who would later turn against Saudi Arabia.

In 1991, Iraq invaded Kuwait and the United States lead a coalition of western and Islamic states to liberate Kuwait. Believing that the whole situation was part of a conspiracy between the United States and the leader of Iraq, Saddam Husseir, especially when some American forces remained in Saudi Arabia after this war, the Afghan Arab formed a coalition among several organizations. Among them were members of revolutionary groups from Egypt "Ayman al-Zawahiri and Mohammad Atef" who urged bin Ladin to finance a wider struggle to overthrow corrupt regimes throughout the Muslim world,[30] and to fight the United States and its presence in the Arabic and Islamic world. Usama Bin laden declared war on the United States and Israel.[31] This coalition is now known as Al- Qa'ida. Bin laden had already joined them--"Ayman al-Zawahiri and Mohammad Atef"--to found Al-Qa'ida, which means "The Base" in Arabic.[32]

Al-Qa'ida first started small attacks against American targets in the region attempting to drive the Americans out of the Arab world by inflicting some casualties among the American troops. They hoped for pressure from the American people on their government to withdraw from the Saudi Arabia. These attacks did not affect the American presence in Saudi Arabia. Al-Qa'ida changed its strategy and attacked United States' embassies in Africa. Finally, on the morning of September 11, 2001, the crime of the century was committed against the United States of America when three of four hijacked civilian commercial airliners crashed into both towers of the World Trade Center in New York City, and the Pentagon in Washington, D.C. The fourth plane crashed in a field in southwestern Pennsylvania before it reached its target. In all, over three thousand innocent people were killed in this attack. Evidence exists that Al- Qa'ida was responsible for this attack.

COUNTERING "ISLAMIC" EXTREMISM

The scholars of the Islamic movements in the Islamic world preach against most of the political and ideological theories from secularism, communism, nationalism and socialism. All of these systems that have been practiced in the Arabic and the Islamic world have failed to bring the Islamic world back to glory. The only thing that will bring the lost glory of Islam is going back to Islam. But the Islam they are calling for is their own interpretation of the Islamic faith, an Islam tailored to fit their goals. The risk here is that with the frustration in the Islamic world, they will establish a large base of support especially among the young generations.

The only way to counter this type of extremism is by finding the reasons for it and treating the causes of it, not the result (the violence). The root of the extremism is based either on political conflict or social injustice, not the differences in the religions. This extremism will not disappear from the Islamic world until real democracy is established in the Islamic world. The Arabic and Islamic countries must fix their political systems. It is the responsibility of the international community to encourage the Arabs governments to establish democratic programs that will educate the public to accept democracy as a way of political life. The tenets of Islam do not contradict the tenets of democracy. In fact the first caliph Abu Bakr, was elected in a democratic way by the Muslims in Medina after the death of the prophet Mohamed in 632AD. When Abu Bakr appointed Omar Bin Al-Kataab to be his successor as the second caliph, the Caliph Omar appointed six men to act as a council to elect one of them to be the third caliph. Othman Bin Afan succeeded Omar, after Othman's death. The Muslims of Medina then elected Ali Bin Abetaleb as the fourth caliph. In the first Islamic state there was an Islamic form of democracy, except with the appointment by Abu Bakr of Omar Bin Al-Kataab as the second caliph. But this was necessary due to the political situation of the Islamic nation at the time, needing a leader that could lead the nation in that critical time. Abu Bakr determined that Omar was the man qualified to lead the nation.

The Ummaih dynasty started the first monarchy in the Islamic political system. It used some of the early Islamic scholars to legalize the monarch system with some verses of the holy Quran. From that time on the Islamic states used the monarch system and the Muslim public lost their political rights. Until democratic governments that are elected by the people and working for the people are established, the political violence is likely to continue.

The Arab and the Islamic states must look into the curriculum's which advocate violence against others, which are taught in schools and universities. They must emphasize the great teaching of Islam and the holy Quran:

"And I will not worship that which ye have been wont to worship, Nor will ye worship that which I worship. To you be your Way, and to me mine."[33]

To establish a good foundation of good relations based on respect and trust and that all humans are brothers, the Quran states:

"O mankind! We created you from a single (pair) of a male and a female, and made you into nations and tribes, that ye may know each other (not that ye may despise each other). Verily the most honoured of you in the sight of Allah is (he who is) the most righteous of you. And Allah has full Knowledge and is well-acquainted (with all things)."[34]

It is also the duty of the international community, led by the United States of America as a world leader, to promote a stable Middle East as important to international political and economical interests. In turn, its allies in the Middle East expect the United States to work sincerely in finding a solution for the Palestinian-Israeli conflict with a fair solution that satisfies both parties.

Today most of western perceptions of the Arabs and the Islamic worlds are derived from the early European Christian scholars and writers sponsored by the church. They brought to the Christian public a negative image of the Arabs, Islam and the Muslim world. The evidence of the hostility against the Arabs go back deep in the early dates. St.Paul's Epistles in the New Testament condemn Ismail (Ishmael) and his descendants even more vehemently than the Old Testament.[35] It was an effort to separate the Christians of Western Europe from Islam in Spain.

In the United States, both the Administration and the public, show a preference for Israel over the Arab nations. This prejudice existed prior to the substantial involvement of the United States in international affairs, and way before it had been under attack from the Muslim militants. The western media often has questionable profit and political motives. In an endless effort to gain support for Israel, it emphasizes stereotypes about the Arabs and Islam. It attempts to implant in the minds of the west a growing danger is Islam and the Arabs. Because negative images often have been assimilated subconsciously, many Westerners are unaware of the deeper causes for their latent hostility toward the Arabs and Muslims.[36] In the 1970s the western media took advantage of the lack of an Arab and Islamic international means to reach the western public. Arabs have also been woefully ignorant of the mechanisms under which the Western media operates to explain their case, positions and interests in the West. They also tend to lack reputable spokespeople in the Western media. Having few active political constituencies in the West, the Arabs have traditionally failed to exert extensive political influence in Europe and the United States.[37] In the Arab-Israeli conflict, the Arabs failed to show the Israeli aggression and crimes that were committed against the Arabs in Palestine. The Western media showed Israel as the underdog that was fighting for its survival. It showed the Arabs as the hostile force that was trying to throw the Israelis in to the sea. Consequently, the Arab side of the Arab-Israeli conflict, as well as other issues of vital interest in the nations in both the Middle East and the West, have not been widely publicized. Thus, it is not at all surprising that the Arab side has rarely, if ever, been given sympathetic attention in the mass electronic and print media of the West.[38]

After the fall of the Soviet Union, which brought an end to the Cold War, and before the tragic attack on the United States that took place on September 11, 2001 by Islamic militants, there was a congressional hearing over the military spending in the United States of America. Former US Secretary of Defence, Robert McNamara, in his 1989 testimony before the Senate Budget Committe stated that defence spending could safely be cut in half over five years.[39]

The United States and West started to search for a new enemy. To the United States, an outside enemy was an essential factor to keep the unity of the American public and to justify high levels of military spending. There were several choices for devising an external enemy and one of them is Islam. The fear of Islam was already in the hearts and minds of Western societies. Western politicians started to send messages to the public, in which they emphasized that the coming threat is the Islamic threat or the Green Peril in an indication to Islam. Former United States Vice President Dan Quayle at a 1990 conference in Washington listed Islam with Nazism and Communism as the challenges the Western civilization must undertake to meet collectively. [40]

But, since the Islamic world is too weak to pose a real threat to the West, the alternative is the portrayal of the Islamic militant as a threat. Today Islamic militant is used to justify high military expenditures when the traditional enemy has disappeared, and the United States and the West is objectively no longer threatened by large scale conventional war or a massive nuclear exchange. Fundamentalism has not been invented by Western politicians but is being used by them. The media has picked up this theme and escalated a campaign in the daily newspapers, weekly magazines, on television news and shows, movies and books that become best sellers, in which they portray Islamic terrorism, and the Muslims as terrorists. While portraying Muslims as enemies of the West and modern societies, they portray Israel as the defender of Westerns societies. The result is the marking of several Arab and Islamic States as terrorist states or states that harbor terrorism.

14

Some Western scholars try to analyze the reasons of the conflict between the West and Islam, in the following manner. First there was the loss of domination of the world to the advancing West.[41] Even if there is some truth in this statement it doesn't explain the hate to the level of war. Islam has lost territory not only to the West, it has also lost territory to the Russians, Chinese and Indians.

The second reasoning of Western scholars was the undermining of Muslim authority in their own countries through the invasion of foreign ideals and ways of life, sometimes through the influence of foreign rulers or settlers.[42] In this statement the authors try to deny the right of the Muslims to live an independent life under their own government rather than living under the occupation of foreign rulers. These authors also forget or try to cover the fact that the West supported most of the activist Islamic groups in the former Soviet Union Islamic nations in the past.

Third, other Western scholars focus on the perceived challenge to Islamic mastery of their own houses from "emancipated women" and "rebellious children".[43] This focus is far from reality. These authors argue that the changes in the Muslim culture and society are the causes of the conflict between Islam and the West. They forget that the Muslim world consists of diverse and different ethnic groups and cultures. A number of Western scholars appear to ignore the period of the Crusades and into modern times. Islam coexisted with other religions within its boundaries. For the last fourteen centuries, Arabs, Christians, and Jews lived under the protection of the Islamic states. The only persecution for Jews and orthodox Christian was carried out on the hands of the European crusaders. The Jewish communities were dreaming of a Messianic revival and were disillusioned by being massacred in Jerusalem along with the Muslim by the Christian crusaders.[44] The Christian catholic (Westerner) crusaders did not recognize (Eastern) orthodox Christianity. In fact the Islamic world was a safe haven for the European Jews. The Ottoman Empire was the haven of Jews fleeing the persecution and the terror of the "holy inquisition" of the Western Christian Catholic Church in Europe.[45]

The Islamic state and Europeans coexisted for fourteen centuries as neighbours with alternating periods of peace and war. The Muslims saw the Europeans as an equal opponent. This view did not rise to the level of hating them for their race or religion. Islam and Christianity have lived side by side-always as neighbors, often as rivals, sometimes as enemies.[46]

The relation of the West and the Islamic world must be restored by dialogue between Islamic nongovernmental organizations (NGOs) and its counterparts in the West, such as universities and strategic research institutes that study Islam. This dialogue will not be intended

15

to decide who is right or who is wrong. It must concentrate on how to bring the two sides to a mutual agreement, an agreement that will put an end to the mutual hatred. The Quran states:

> "And argue not with the people of the Scripture (Jews and Christians), unless it be in (a way) that is better (with good words and in good manner, inviting them to Islâmic Monotheism with His Verses), except with such of them as do wrong, and say (to them): "We believe in that which has been revealed to us and revealed to you; our Ilâh (God) and your Ilâh (God) is One (i.e. Allâh), and to Him we have submitted (as Muslims)."[17]

It is the responsibility of the scholars and religious leaders from both sides to correct their respective images of the other side. There must be a unity of effort between the Islamic world and international community to fight the poverty in the Islamic world, in an effort to raise the standard of living, health, and education.

CONCLUSION

The issue of terrorism and Islam is a complex one. The policies that are formulated for combating, preventing, or treating terrorism that has Islamic roots or origins cannot rely on the simplistic stereotypes that are portrayed in the Western print and electronic media. They often have serious underlying profit motives or their own political agendas. Both the West and the Islamic countries must face up to the issue of terrorism in a balanced and multifaceted fashion. Indeed, the media campaign that the United States has launched in the Arab and Islamic world often lacks a sense of realism and even-handedness. Indeed, it does not matter to Arab audiences whether Muslims in the United States can lead "normal lives" and freely attend Islamic schools. When a United States made and Israeli modified M-60A3/A5 Sabra tanks shells with impunity Palestinian residential neighborhoods and schools in the occupied West Bank, it is bad for relations.

The international community must seriously address the issues discussed above with honesty and open-mindedness. Rightly or wrongly, it falls upon the United States as a leader in the international community to take the lead in discussing the issues, and by example, enacting the solutions.

Through the passage of time the basics and beauty of Islam, one of the heavenly religions, has been twisted and used for the advantage of those corrupted by power. In this sense, it has become a victim of terrorism, and is not the cause of terrorism. Unfortunately, it may not achieve world-wide acceptance if the United States, as international leader and a

16

nation founded on religious freedom, does not lead the effort to accept the tenets of Islam and accommodate its sincere followers.

WORD COUNT = 7,606

ENDNOTES

[1] Maryam Jameelah,Islam versus Ahl Al Kitab, Taj Company 1989.P1

[2] Maryam Jameelah,Islam versus Ahl Al Kitab, Taj Company 1989.P33

[3] Maryam Jameelah,Islam versus Ahl Al Kitab, Taj Company 1989.P33

[4] Safi-ur-Rahman Al-Mubarakpuri, AR-RAHEEQ AL-MAKHTUM(THE SEALED NECTAR) P34

[5] Safi-ur-Rahman Al-Mubarakpuri, AR-RAHEEQ AL-MAKHTUM(THE SEALED NECTAR) P37

[6] The holy Quran.39:3

[7] Maryam Jameelah,Islam versus Ahl Al Kitab, Taj Company 1989.P35

[8] The holy Quran.2:190

[9] Bernard Lewis, Islam and the west, Oxford University Press 1993.P4

[10] The holy Quran.2:256

[11] Abdelnasser The Islamic movement in Egypt, Kegan Paul Int. P20-21

[12] The holy Quran.4:113, 4:114, 4:115

[13] Abdelnasser The Islamic movement in Egypt, Kegan Paul Int. P20

[14] Bernard Lewis, Islam and the west, Oxford University Press 1993. P155

[15] Dr. Ahmed Refat & Dr. Salih Al-Taiar "International terror" EURO-ARABIC Studies Centre 1998

[16] The holy Quran.2:205

[17] The holy Quran.5:33

[18] Ralph Peters, Rolling Back Radical Islam, PARAMETERS VOL.XXXII,NO.3 Autumn 2002,P8

[19] Khalid Aiyed Palestine encyclopaedia second section sixth vol. First edition Beirut. P549-550

[20] Asharq al-Awsat Newspaper, Arabic Issue ,16November 2002 Vol.25 No.8754

[21] Bernard Lewis, Islam and the west, Oxford University Press 1993. P139

[22] Abdelnasser The Islamic movement in Egypt, Kegan Paul Int. P33

[23] Ralph Peters, Rolling Back Radical Islam, PARAMETERS VOL.XXXII,NO.3 Autumn 2002,P8

[24] Abdelnasser The Islamic movement in Egypt, Kegan Paul Int. P85

[25] David G. Kibble, The attacks of 9/11:Evidence of a Clash of Religions, PARAMETERS VOL.XXXII,NO.3 Autumn 2002, P38

[26] Abdus Sattar Ghazali, ISLAM IN THE POST-COLD WAR ERA

[27] Ziad Abu-Amr, Islamic Fundamentalism in the West Bank and Gaza, Indiana University press 1984, Pxvi

[28] http://www.geocities.com/HotSprings/Spa/3606/binladen.html

[29] Abdus Sattar Ghazali, ISLAM IN THE POST-COLD WAR ERA

[30] http://www.publiceye.org/frontpage/911/Islam/rosenfeld2001-01.htm#TopOfPage

[31] http://www.suite101.com/article.cfm/3874/79804 Usamah Bin Ladin – Terrorism's Poster Boy Rick Francona update of an article,

[32] http://www.publiceye.org/frontpage/911/Islam/rosenfeld2001-01.htm#TopOfPage

[33] The holy Quran. 109:4,5, and6

[34] The holy Quran. 49:13

[35] Maryam Jameelah, Islam versus Ahl Al Kitab, Taj Company 1989.P32

[36] Janice J.Terry, Mistaken Identity Arab Stereotypes in Popular Writing, American-Arab Affairs Council,1985 ,P12

[37] Janice J.Terry, Mistaken Identity Arab Stereotypes in Popular Writing, American-Arab Affairs Council,1985 ,P12

[38] Janice J.Terry, Mistaken Identity Arab Stereotypes in Popular Writing, American-Arab Affairs Council,1985 ,P12

[39] Abdus Sattar Ghazali, ISLAM IN THE POST-COLD WAR ERA

[40] Abdus Sattar Ghazali, ISLAM IN THE POST-COLD WAR ERA

[41] Chaplain (LTC) John P. Hash, ISLAMIC RADICAL AND TERROR AGINST THE WEST, USAWC.2002 P9

[42] Chaplain (LTC) John P. Hash, ISLAMIC RADICAL AND TERROR AGINST THE WEST, USAWC.2002 P9

[43] Chaplain (LTC) John P. Hash, ISLAMIC RADICAL AND TERROR AGINST THE WEST, USAWC.2002 P9

[44] Maryam Jameelah, Islam versus Ahl Al Kitab, Taj Company 1989.P7

[45] Maryam Jameelah, Islam versus Ahl Al Kitab, Taj Company 1989.P8

[46] Bernard Lewis, Islam and the west, Oxford University Press 1993. preface

[47] The holy Quran.11:45